The SIMPLE guide to Property Developing

Robert Colvin

Copyright © 2016 Robert Colvin

All rights reserved, including the right to reproduce this book, or portions thereof in any form. No part of this text may be reproduced, transmitted, downloaded, decompiled, reverse engineered, or stored, in any form or introduced into any information storage and retrieval system, in any form or by any means, whether electronic or mechanical without the express written permission of the author.

ISBN: 978-1-326-82387-0

PublishNation
www.publishnation.co.uk

Preface

I was brought up in South East London, a place I still live today. My parents had very little money which could explain my hunger for wanting more. They worked tirelessly to provide myself and my siblings with as much as possible.

When I was only 14 years old my dad sadly passed away, my brother who is slightly older than me had recently started working Saturdays as a labourer on a building site. My mum thought it would be a great distraction for me if I could join him. He wasn't best keen on the idea but was obviously persuaded. Mums have that ability. From day one I loved it. I was a digger, mixer, mover and of course tea boy. For the next two years I worked every Saturday and most school holidays, learning as much as I could.

After completing my GCSEs the building firm offered me a full time carpentry apprenticeship. I jumped at the chance. My hard work had paid off. I was enrolled onto a college course to which I attended two days every fortnight. For the next three years I learnt every aspect of building. We renovated houses, built extensions, created new builds and even built swimming pools.

When I was 18 I applied for a job in the London Fire Brigade. I'd always wanted to do something to help people, and this was my chance. To my amazement I passed all the written and physical tests and was accepted into the Brigade. After completing my three years' probation, I was granted permission to have a second job. A lot of Firefighters do this to enhance their wage. It was then I registered as a self-employed carpenter, brought myself a small Citroen Berlingo van and went it alone. I loved the independence of meeting clients, pricing jobs and completing them.

At the age of 21 I was able to combine my Firefighter and building salaries with my then girlfriend and now wife's NHS income to borrow enough money to fund our first project.

We instantly got the property developing bug, and still to this day enjoy every aspect of developing. We work for so much of our lives, it's vitally important to enjoy every day. I truly believe you can too.

Chapters

Introduction
Know Your Market
Know What and How to Buy
How to Choose a Builder
Pre Plan
The Template
Don't Get Personal
Loft Converting
Kitchen Extending
Side Extending
Fully Refurbishing
Driveways & Gardens
How to Sell Your Development.

Introduction

The thought of renovating a tired unloved property, bringing it back to life and selling on for a large profit appeals to many and sounds easy, and truth be told it is. However I have seen want to be property developers make some simple mistakes which have cost them dearly.

If a property sits on the market for six months and just won't sell, there is something very wrong. A successful development is one that the first person who walks through the door wants to buy, and most importantly makes you money, lots of money. Every property I have ever extended and developed has sold the same week it goes on the market, and by following my simple methods within this book, I'm going to show you how easy it is.

Millions of people around the world are happy paying their monthly mortgage payments year in, year out until the twenty five or thirty five years in some cases are up. I am not saying for one minute there is a problem with this, my own mother was very content doing exactly that. However it was not something I wanted to do. I wanted disposable income, and I wanted choice. I've always said that it's not the money that makes people happy, it's the choices it gives you, and if you make the right ones, you can be incredibly happy indeed.

I like earning money and I certainly like spending money. I feel money should be enjoyed in whichever way makes you happy, whether that be holidaying with friends and family or buying that sports car or handbag you have always wanted.

One of the first things you will need to do in order to succeed is believe in yourself. By purchasing this book, you have already started that process, and for that I believe in you.

Know Your Market

Before buying your development, research the surrounding area. The questions you should be asking yourself are:

How good are the transport links? Where's the nearest shop? What's the crime rate? Are there schools? If so primary or secondary, what is the catchment area? How good are they? Check the OFSTED report. All these things can be checked from the comfort of your sofa in less than ten minutes. When looking on the large property marketing websites, there are links to follow that give you all the above information at the click of a button.

Primary School catchment areas have dramatically decreased in recent years, bumping up property prices in the school surrounding areas.

I once found out that a primary school in my home town was lowering their catchment area from a mile to half a mile when the new term time began. I found a dated un-extended 3 bedroom semi-detached property within the new designated catchment area and totally renovated it, adding both a large kitchen extension and loft conversion. I knew my market was going to be a young family with 2 or 3 children and a car or two. I had painted a picture in my mind of whom I was aiming the property at. With all that in mind I designed a family home that would be perfect for all of the above.

Adding the loft conversion made an impressive master bedroom with en suite bathroom. It had views overlooking the park and woodland to which the property backed onto. I added a large kitchen extension with pitched roof and Velux windows. This added height to the room and flooded it with light. It had bi-fold doors leading to the garden, a large kitchen island with built in appliances, tiled floor for easy cleaning for when the family came back from the woods, room for a large sofa and TV, it also had room for a dining table. I managed to add a downstairs toilet and utility room as well as off road parking. A combination of all these things ticked all the boxes that a growing family would need. I had created the perfect family home. It was from this development I made my template. I knew it worked. The house went on the market and the first people who walked through the door brought it, and for well over the asking price as well.

Breakdowns of the costs are as follows.

Market Price of the Property	£275,000.00
Purchase Price	£268,000.00
Renovation Cost including Mortgage payments	£64,000.00
Market price once renovated	£400,000.00
Resale Price	£420,000.00
Profit	£88,000.00

I wouldn't of done all those things to the property had it not been in that school catchment area. I just wouldn't of got my money back. I would have added the kitchen extension to add that wow factor but would not have added the extra bedroom and bathroom in the loft.

Know your area and know your potential buyers. If I was aiming a property at a young professional couple who work in the city, it would need to be walking distance to a station. It would need to be modern, contemporary and easy to maintain. I doubt I would add the expense and time of a driveway. Ask yourself whether they would own a car. The garden would need to be low maintenance; I personally would consider adding artificial grass. The last thing a young city worker wants to do is spend their weekends weeding the garden. They want to be entertaining.

It's worth remembering that planning permission is not always granted, so make sure you have done your research on the surrounding properties. If the neighbouring properties have similar extensions and conversions, chances are that you will get the permission granted too. If you didn't for whatever reason, you would have a case against the council for an appeal.

Most councils now allow something called "Permitted Development Rights" which allows householders to improve and extend their homes without the need to apply for planning permission. There are many constraints to adhere to, however it can be a very quick and easy way to extend your property.

Planning permission in most cases can take between ten and twelve weeks. If you have a mortgage on the property this valuable time could be eating into your profit margin, so Permitted Development Rights really can save valuable pounds.

Local building control officers and planning officers are normally more than happy to help you establish what process is best suited to your property. If your property is in an area of outstanding natural beauty or has other covenants surrounding it, it can affect the permitted development rights. It's vital you establish which process is correct as the last thing you would want to do is tear down your new extension, costing you some or all of your profit margin.

Know What and How to Buy

Knowing what to buy and getting your development for the right price is vital. It's no good paying over the odds for a property leaving little or no room for profit. Every time I leave my house I'm on the lookout for potential money making properties. One of the main things I look for in a development are damaged original wooden window frames. This is a tell-tale sign that the property has not been modernised in a long time if not ever. If the windows are original I almost guarantee that everything else is too.

Looking at the roof is also a great way to tell if the property has been updated. If not then you are in for a treat. These are my favourite properties to buy. Firstly because the condition of the property will be reflected in the price, meaning a bargain can be had and secondly it's easier and cheaper to start from scratch then it is to try and rectify a bodged job. If you find one of these properties on the market book a viewing in quick. If you don't someone else will.

Once you have viewed a property determine what alterations and adaptations you would like to carry out, then research the market to see what similar properties in the local area have sold for. It's a good idea to take your builder with you to the viewings, or certainly to a second viewing, before submitting your offer. That way you will be able to work backwards with the sums ensuring you don't pay over the odds. I would want to earn at least 10% on any development I invested in so use that as a basis.

First impressions go along way when viewing properties, whether it is the estate agent showing you around or the homeowner. I've known sellers to take a lower price because they like the couple viewing it. Always be polite and remember it's their home and to them it's their castle. They may have brought up their children there, and it probably holds great memories. It's no good walking around saying out loud how much you hate the wallpaper or the carpets, it will only upset them. There is no harm mentioning that you would like to put your own mark on the property but you can do that quite easily without being rude. Regardless of the condition of the property ask the homeowner if they would like you to remove your shoes. It's very polite and it shows them you have respect. Nine times out of ten they say no but be prepared to take them off if they say yes. So no wearing your oldest pair of socks with a dozen holes in.

Adding another bedroom will always increase the value of a property, but some areas will increase in value more so than others. Use online property websites to see properties in your area that have sold. Ensure you don't just view properties that are still on the market as this will not give you a true indication of prices. By doing so will help you determine whether to add another bedroom to increase the value or maybe an additional reception room.

Registering your details with local estate agents is a great way to be first in line to a property. If you are buying your development with cash you are in the best position possible to get a great deal on your development, ensuring maximum profits. However not everyone has that luxury. Well not yet at least. After completing just a handful of developments you too could be a cash buyer.

If you are buying your development with a mortgage, ensure you have it agreed in principle. Any good agent will also want to see proof of funds for the property deposit. Without these there is no way an agent will take you seriously, meaning you could miss out on that perfect property. If you have your money safely invested in an ISA, Premium Bonds or any other savings account, ensure you allow enough time for the funds to be transferred out should an offer be accepted. One thing to remember is that mortgage companies will only lend money on a habitual property. This means they will need a working kitchen and bathroom. If you do find a derelict property, I'm sure you will find a mortgage company to lend you the money but be prepared to pay a much higher interest rate.

If you are needing to sell your property in order to purchase your next project, I would advise selling through the agent you would be buying from. This is a great way to secure your next project. It's win win for the agent. They would be getting double commission. Your bargaining tool is that if you don't get the property you have offered on, you will not be selling through them.

It's also a great way to speed up the chain. Having too many agents dealing with a property chain only delays things.

How to Choose a Builder

Finding a reliable, honest, competent builder can be challenging but is no means impossible. The first rule of thumb is to get reliable recommendations. Chat to friends and family to see if they have had any building work carried out. If so would they recommend their builder?

Look around your local area to see if any properties are having work done. Scaffolding around a property is a tell-tale sign that building work is being carried out. Don't be embarrassed to knock on the door and ask the homeowners if they are happy with their builders. They probably did the same thing to find them in the first place. Where possible ask to see the finished result. You wouldn't spend £35,000.00 on a car without looking inside right? They can only say no, and you have lost nothing.

I would always recommend getting at least three quotes from different builders. Don't automatically go with the cheapest quote as there may be a reason why it's cheaper. It may not include certain items, so in the long run could cost you more. Most builders I speak to now use a surveying service that prices their drawing up for them for a reasonably small fee. It works like this; you supply the builder with a set of building regulation drawings that the architect has drawn up. The builder sends them off to the surveyors that have up to date material costing's from local builders merchants. It is so detailed, it even prices in the nails used for the roof tiles. It costs the builder approximately £90.00 to get a set of loft conversion drawings priced up which from my point of view is a price worth paying. Gone are the days where I would sit down for hours on end writing down every building material needed and trying to get accurate prices for them. I would much rather spend the £90.00 and enjoy my time with my family and friends.

I believe good builders are booked up for between 6 months to 2 years so alarm bells should be ringing if a builder can start straight away.

I once built a loft conversion for a young family who had been ripped off by their previous builder. He had taken five months to build what can only be described as a dangerous Wendy house in their loft, costing them £28,000.00.

On my first site inspection I had to secure the roof with temporary supports to ensure the families safety overnight. There should have been a total of seven RSJs (steel supports) in the loft space, they had put in none.

The builder had totally endangered the lives of the family which to me is unforgivable. It cost the family an additional £35,000.00 to completely remove all traces of the previous builders and construct a safe usable bedroom with en suite facilities.

Builds should never go that wrong. It is standard practice that the local authority building inspector will carry out regular site inspections ensuring the building work is being carried out to the current building regulations. I have had clients ask me in the past if they can be present during the building inspector's visits, and I welcome the opportunity. It gives the homeowner so much reassurance when the building inspector signs off each stage of the works, after all it's their money that is being spent and they want to know it's being spent wisely.

Contracts are a must whenever employing a builder to protect yourself and the builder. It needs to be very detailed with the exact extent of the works to be carried out and also include all the stage payment dates.

Under no circumstances will any good builder ask for the full amount of the contract price upfront.

Stage payments are an easy and fair way for the builder to be paid. For example.

Contract price = £35,000.00
Job completion time = 8 Weeks
Deposit = £4,000.00
X7 weekly instalments of £4,000.00
Job completion = £3,000.00
Total = £35,000.00

Each stage should be detailed with the amount of work that will be carried out by the date payment is due. I.e. - end of week one, roof structure complete, end of week two roof fully tiled and so on.

Money should only be released once you are happy these stages are being met. Some architects will inspect the build along the way and carry out the stage payments for you, however this will be a service they will charge for. You should seriously consider this method of payment structure if you will be away on holiday for a few weeks or just too busy to be around to inspect the work carried out by the builders. It's no fair leaving the builder without payment just because you are busy. I once pulled all my guys off a job because the home owners cheque bounced. I know you might think that's a bit harsh but if I had four tradespeople working on £150.00 each a day, after one week I would be out of pocket £3,000.00 plus materials. It has got to be fair both ways. You want a great job done and the builders want to earn a fair living.

Once you have built up a good relationship with your builder, and you're happy with the end result, it's good to stick with them for your next development. Your subsequent builds will flow much easier if you're both singing from the same hymn sheet.

Pre Plan

When I buy a property to refurbish I plan everything down to the last plug socket before I start the refurbishment on day one. On average in the UK it takes ten weeks for a property to come off the market, exchange and complete. This is a perfect time to plan your project. I totally understand that a property can fall through during this time but it's a risk I'm willing to take.

A great way to get ideas for your project is to buy some property magazines. They are not expensive, and over the years I have found them invaluable.

Not only do they give you the ability to visualise the project by showing you the before and after photos, but give you contact information for the various material suppliers. Ensure you make a list of all the materials and suppliers you have found so you can easily refer back to them when you are ready to go. It's also a good idea to make a Mood board so you can collate all the images together to insure they all tie in.

Some property developers will go as far as getting drawings and planning permission done while the solicitors are drawing up the legal documents. I'm not against this, but you would have to be willing to lose that money should the home owner pull out of the sale.

My Architect charges approximately £1,000.00 for a set of building regulation drawings to be completed and for the relevant paperwork to be submitted to the council. My advice would be to wait until the contracts are signed and exchanged. At least that way you know you will not be throwing away money. Exchange of contracts is normally a week before completion so that gives you a little head start. There will be plenty of other work that can be undertaken while you wait for planning permission.

While the legal side is being taken care of, there is no harm in planning such things as kitchen and bathroom layouts. If the estate agent hasn't got accurate room dimensions, book a viewing in with the vendor to carry this out yourself. Every detail planned now will speed up the development, meaning less mortgage payments need to be paid and more profit margin to be spent. Don't go so far as to purchase anything until that legal documentation is completed. You don't want to end up with a £4,000 kitchen and nowhere to put it. I totally understand there may be some changes that need to be made along the way, but at least you have a plan to work from.

Pre planning such things as floor finishes in an extension are vital to the architect's drawings. Depending on the chosen material, the architect will adjust the drawings to comply to current building regulations. This will become more apparent once you have read the kitchen extending chapter. You can of course get the architect to change or amend a set of drawings but be prepaid to pay an hourly fee for this service.

The Template

There's a famous old saying "If a jobs worth doing its worth doing well". If you want to be a successful property developer, make that your new favourite saying.

Over the past 17 years I have seen hundreds of examples of poor workmanship, and it saddens me that with a little more care and not a lot more money it could have been done ten times better.

The main culprit for this is decorating. So many people think they are the new Pablo Picasso and that decorating a whole house just needs a trip to the local DIY store and a few evenings and weekends of persistence. I understand that money towards the end of a refurbishment is tight but all your hard earned work and potential profit could be diminishing.

If you have employed the best plasterer in the world, once an amateur decorator has slapped on the paint it can ruin the pristine finish he or she has left. I have seen skirting and architrave mouldings disappear due to the large volumes of paint applied.

My advices to you is work overtime and weekends to pay a decorator. Many people make the mistake of doing certain jobs themselves when in fact it would have worked out cheaper to get the trades in.

For example if you are earning £120 a day in your current job and a tradesperson is charging you £150 a day but completing the job in half the time and to a much higher specification you are quids in. The painting is the first thing a potential buyer is going to see as they walk through the door, don't let them pick faults. The property should be immaculate if you want to get top money for it on completion.

I tend to get my decorators to paint everything bar the hallway and bathroom in White. Painting the walls and ceilings white gives a sense of space and light. It's clean and natural. I am NOT a lover of Magnolia. It's so dated and just doesn't fit into the look I go for in my properties.

I tend to get the hallway decorated in a light Grey. It adds a bit of class to a property, I also find it ties in all the rooms off of it. I use a soft sheen on the hallway walls. It allows the light to bounce off it and also is easy wipe clean should you mark it, I'm sure if you have children you often find hand prints scattered around the hall. Nothing that a little wet wipe can't sort out.

High specification does not necessarily mean high cost. Cheap carpets look cheap but look out for the 50% sales. Large carpet showrooms seem to have one every week. I've also found that I can save a small fortune buying my underlay and gripper rods (short lengths of timber with nails poking out, that secures the carpet around the edge of a room) on the internet using trade websites. Carpet showrooms charge around £10 - £15 per square meter for a good quality carpet underlay, I can buy it online for £1.50, that's a saving of around £600 on a standard three bed semi. I'm sure you can already think what you could buy with that £600 saving, and if you're not, you should be. That's the way you need to train your brain to think, it will make you maximise your profits.

Bathroom

I mentioned I painted bathrooms. Some of you reading this might be thinking why I don't fully tile a bathroom, floor to ceiling and here is why. Cheap tiles look cheap. If you were too fully tile a bathroom in cheap tiles potential buyers would spot it a mile off. It just doesn't give that wow factor you want to achieve.

You are much better off buying a much nicer, better quality tile but using less of them. Use them to tile around your bath, shower and hand basin. The rest of the walls can be painted. Steer away from tiles that are naturally porous and need sealing constantly. It's something that potential buyers may not like. Remember, you're selling the dream home and getting a paint brush out every six months to paint your bathroom tiles with a sealer certainly isn't in any of my dreams. If you're unsure which tiles need sealing, the salesperson in your local tile dealership will be able to advise you.

Under floor heating is not a must but it can be an added selling point. It can cost as little as £200 to install under floor heating in a bathroom, and in today's society everybody loves a gadget. If you were to install it, make sure the tiles and adhesive you buy are compatible. The last thing you want is to turn it on and the whole floor starts to crack. One thing I would say is if you do install it, turn it on during your selling open day whether it's a cold day outside or not. I personally make everyone take their shoes off when I show them around properties for two reasons. Firstly it shows you have pride in your property, and don't want to get it ruined. If the potential buyers think you have pride in your carpets, they are going to think you have pride in the rest of your development. And secondly so they can feel the warmth from your under floor heating. I can almost guarantee at least one person will say " oh that will be lovely getting out the bath and standing on that". Remember, you are selling a dream and for that one moment, that potential buyer was dreaming.

Lighting in a bathroom can be very important. There are two places in a home I believe spotlights work, one of which is the bathroom. I always buy the brushed chrome effect spotlights. I think the white and polished chrome ones can look cheap and tacky. For me, pull cord switches are a no go. This is another way to ruin the look of a bathroom. Where possible, position the switch on the outside of the bathroom, eliminating the need for a pull cord. Also potential buyers with young children would see instant fault. Don't put any doubt in the buyer's minds.

All bathrooms need an extractor fan to comply to building regulations. There are hundreds to choose from on the market but let me save you the time in searching. Buy a slim line white, ceiling mounted fan. They blend in nicely with the white panted ceiling, taking your eye off them.

When buying bathroom suites, try buying each item from the same manufacture. I have found in the past that the porcelain shading can vary between manufacturers. Truth be told most people wouldn't notice, but I would and that's good enough reason for me.

Kitchen

Kitchens can be the most expensive part of a property refurbishment, however you can achieve a sleek elegant look without breaking the bank. There is one main bit of advice I would give when it comes to choosing kitchen units and that is "Pick White". White kitchens don't go out of fashion, they look clean and tidy and ninety nine per cent of people like them.

Personally I would recommend a While Gloss plain flush kitchen unit door with solid oak worktops. The combination works very well together. The light bounces off the gloss cabinet doors giving the kitchen a sense of space and light. The oak worktops once treated with clear teak oil give a sense of class and elegance. I always find it cheaper to buy the worktops online. They tend to be of a better quality and much cheaper. Ensure you buy 40mm thick worktops. They do sell them in 28mm but it looks cheap. The price difference is minimal. If your budget allows, marble or granite can add the wow factor to any kitchen but it can be expensive. See how your budget goes.

There are some amazing coloured kitchens out there but please remember, you are doing this to sell and make money. Personal preference does not come in to this. Another great thing about white kitchens is they tend to be one of the cheapest.

Tiling above the kitchen worktop can finish of the elegant look nicely. Some people choose to have an oak up-stand instead, but I would advise to use a white Metro tile. They are very reasonable in price and fit nicely in any home.

I'm not a lover of metal plug sockets anywhere in a property, especially the kitchen. If you are going for a white kitchen and white tiles, it only makes sense to buy white plug sockets too. Ensure you have allowed for enough sockets into your kitchen design. Make a list of all the kitchen electrical appliances that tend to be used at worktop level such as a kettle and toaster. Any keen cook will notice things like that straight away. Although I don't like metal plug sockets, I do like brushed chrome light switches. These can make each room look classy. I mentioned that there are two places I use spotlight in a property. The second is the kitchen. Don't make your kitchen ceiling look like an airport runway by installing too many. It's really over powering. Ensure you buy brushed chrome spotlights to tie in with the light switches and potentially the kitchen unit handles. That's if your kitchen range has handles. Some popular kitchens on the market today have integrated handles which I really like.

I tend to install a dimmer switch in the kitchen, so the lighting can be turned down when the mood allows. If buying a dimmer switch, make sure you buy spotlights that are compatible as not all of them are. Your local electrical wholesalers will be more than happy to advise you.

Islands in a kitchen are what people dream of. Designing an island into a kitchen really can give a wow factor. Your local DIY retailer and individual kitchen companies are normally more than happy to sit down with you and design your kitchen with the hope you will buy it. Get a few quotes from different retailers as prices really can vary. Independent kitchen fitters will also be more than happy to design your kitchen. I almost guarantee they will supply and fit a kitchen much cheaper than any large retailer. Once again, insure you have sourced genuine recommendations before choosing a kitchen fitter. It's an incredibly important part of the property renovation and you want it fitted well.

In the internet age we live in, kitchen appliances are almost certainly cheaper brought online. I wouldn't recommend buying the cheapest of the cheap but I also wouldn't recommend spending half your refurbishment budget on them either. Mid-range appliances are fine.

I recommend installing a gas hob where possible and an electric oven, double if your budget allows. My research shows that 90% of households prefer cooking with a gas hob and electric oven. You are aiming your property refurbishment at the masses so give them what they want. The chrome or black appliance surrounds can vary in shade between the manufactures so I would recommend buying all the same make appliances so they all tie in together nicely. Make sure you keep all the receipts, as they normally come with a one or two year warranty and this is great selling point. I always make up a folder to show potential buyers on the open day with all relevant paperwork in. Not only the kitchen appliances but window certificates and building regulation completion certificates really help. It gives potential buyers piece of mind that the house and everything in it isn't going to go bang the minute they get the keys.

Bedrooms

Bedrooms should be kept very plain. Again I paint them white to maximise the look of the room.

Think about the position a bed should go within the room because this will help you decide the locations of the electrical sockets. It's pointless having a plug socket behind the bed where it's inaccessible. I would always fit four or five double sockets in a bedroom depending on the size. Don't waste your money on expensive chrome or brass faced sockets. Once the room is furnished they will be somewhat out of site. Why spend £15.00 on an electrical socket when you could spend £3.00.

Most people whether you agree with it or not have a television in their bedrooms, ensure you allow for a TV areal socket. These little details can be pointed out to potential buyers when you're showing them around. I personally go that extra step further and get cables run in the wall for Sky Television.

Building regulations specify that any habitable rooms such as bedrooms need to have an escape window that can open enough to allow a person to climb through should they need to escape from fire. It is vitally important that you comply with this. All good window companies will fit these windows as standard but it's worth checking for peace of mind.

I also ensure I fit fire doors to all rooms except bathrooms. You might think it's an un-justified added cost but you would be wrong. All my years in the Fire Brigade have shown me that fire doors really do save lives. It's a cost I am always willing to spend. If you are considering a loft conversion on the property, current building regulations stipulate that fire doors must be fitted to all habitable rooms anyway so it's a job that needs to be done. I've found that potential buyers also find it a great comfort, which I don't blame them.

Lounge

Lounges should be a haven. A place where you can unwind at the end of a day, with a glass of wine. They need to be warm and inviting. I would always recommend a carpet as a floor covering. I feel that a solid floor such as Oak or tiles would make the room feel cold. Carpets in any room tend to add that cosy feeling.

If the room has a chimney breast, I feel that a fireplace is a must. It doesn't necessarily have to be operational but it really adds warmth and character to a room. There are fantastic replica fireplaces on the market if an original is unobtainable. Ensure you purchase the correct fireplace to suit the properties era. A simple web search can help you find the correct style for your property. I recently brought a 1930s replica fireplace for £480.00 which I was incredibly happy with. It totally transformed the room, and everyone who walks in the room comments on it.

Ensure you get your electrician to wire an aerial and possibly a Sky TV socket into the room. Try and work out the best layout for furniture and position the aerial socket accordingly.

Utility room

If a utility room can be fitted into a property then please do so. It doesn't have to be massive in size, but large enough to satisfy. A utility room is there to serve a purpose, to keep the washing machine out the way, along with your dirty laundry. And I'm sure we have all acquired some of that over the years. It also acts as a sound barrier. When hosting a dinner party, the last thing you want to hear in the background is the washing machine spinning at 1200 RPM

Ideally it would also house a tumble drier but this is an added bonus, not a must. Its good practice to fit a cupboard in, to store all the washing powders etc. If you currently live in a property with a utility room, I'm sure you will agree it would now be hard to live without.

Garden

If you remember Ground Force with Alan Titchmarsh, you will remember how creative and luxurious gardens can be. That said it's not an area I would spend excessive sums of money on. I certainly wouldn't advise adding a pond or water feature. Anyone with small children would instantly see this as a negative, and you only want to be creating positives. Keep the garden plain, with plenty of grass and a decent size patio. By decent I recommend approximately 3 meters from the back of the house and about 5 meters wide. That's plenty big enough for a table and chairs. Remember patio slabs are more expensive than grass, so the larger you make it, the more its eating into your profit margin. If the garden fences are tatty I would recommend replacing them. Make sure you chat to your neighbours about this before you start as lots of disputes are caused by something as simple as a fence being on their land by 2mm. There is every possibility the neighbours will pay half towards the fence saving you even more money.

If using fence panels, which is by far the cheapest method of fencing, stay away from the fancy curvy decorative panels. Firstly they are extremely expensive but also they are not to everyone's taste. Keep the panels plain and simple.

I don't believe you need to go to the expense of installing a garden shed. They can end up being quite expensive and I don't think someone is going to be put off by not having one. If it's a small garden it will also make it look smaller. It's something they can add later if they wish. Once the property has been sold the new owners may wish to totally transform the garden, but at least they have a blank canvas to work from.

Don't Get Personal

Getting personal is the easiest way of dwindling away your profit margin. And truth be told I'm guilty of this in the past but pleased to say I have learnt my lesson. You could potentially get personal with just about every aspect of your development whether it is carpets, colours or bathroom wall tiles. You might have the most extravagant taste but keep in the forefront of your mind that you are doing this to sell. It has got to appeal to the majority of people.

Let's say your favourite colour is Red, and you're thinking of painting one of the bedrooms in this lovely passionate colour. My advice to you is don't. Paint it White. And this is why. The human brain finds it harder to remove a colour from a picture than to add one. Painter's canvasses are White for a reason. It's not just as a base layer, it allows the brain to paint its own picture. By painting a room a pacific colour you are limiting your potential buyers, as not everyone can see the bigger picture. They will automatically get a negative view on the property. By painting it white, it's very easy for potential buyers to visualise their own colour preference.

Picking the right colour carpets can also be quite challenging. Personally I stay away from the very dark colours like brown, and the very light colours such as cream. Dark carpets can make the room look smaller than it actually is and very light carpets are just screaming disaster with regards to stains. You can ask the salesperson in the carpet shop which is a best seller but be careful they don't sell you a very expensive range. I tend to pick either a biscuit colour carpet or a Grey. Both these colours go well with white walls and ensure the room sizes are shown to the best of their ability. The same principle applies to hard floor coverings such as wood and tiles. Stick to a mid-colour to ensure maximum appeal. I recently viewed a property with dark Mahogany flooring throughout, and even on a bright sunny day the house looked dull.

If you are struggling to make decisions throughout your development, try looking at some new build properties either on the internet or in person. Large building firms and developers employ interior designers to appeal to the mass market. It's not often a new build property doesn't sell unless it is massively over-priced. Once you have your first development under your belt you will feel much more confident making decisions on the next one. That's after you have treated yourself to a little holiday with some of your profit of course.

Loft Converting

I understand that not everyone can afford to buy a second property to renovate, extend and sell on for large profits. Adding square footage onto your current property can dramatically increase the value of your home.

According to property experts, adding a loft conversion onto your current home can increase the value by as much as 20%. I have built many loft conversions over the years not just on my own properties but for clients as well.

Depending on location, a standard loft conversion that adds an additional bedroom with en suite bathroom would cost the homeowner approx. £30,000.00.

So let's do the sums -

Current property value=£380,000.00
Loft Conversion build cost=£30,000.00
New property value with 20% increase=£456,000.00
Profit =£46,000.00

So by getting a team of experienced builders into extend your home has just made you a potential £46,000.00 profit in six to eight weeks with not lifting a finger. Well you may have to make a few cups of tea and buy some biscuits. Not bad if you ask me. That is nearly double the average UK yearly wage. Now imagine doing two of these a year.

Most homeowners in the UK pay their mortgages off into their late 50s and early 60s. Wouldn't it be nice to pay your mortgage off in two years? It truly can happen. All this can be done whilst carrying out your current job, your life doesn't have to alter if you don't want it to. Just imagine the choices you would have once you no longer have a Mortgage to worry about. The holidays you could have, the cars you could buy or the family you could treat? The possibilities are endless.

I understand that moving home two or three times a year could be stressful, however there are things you can do to minimise your stress. Utilising self-storage facilities to store away the furniture and belongings you only use once in a blue moon can lower your removal costs and make that move quicker and easier. Also by hiring a professional removal company to take the load off of you and your family would be wise.

When I've built loft conversions for clients their main concern was the work intruding on their home life. Any professional builder will do their very best not to disrupt your home and family. Inform your builders of your concerns at the very beginning so they can make arrangement to meet your needs.

I always hired portable toilets for my workforce and storage facility's if needed. On average there are 4 trades' people on site every day, and the last thing a homeowner wants is them disrupting the families' routines. With the right forward planning it really doesn't have too.

When planning a loft conversion either on your current home or on a development project, ensure you budget in the cost of new roof tiles. Obviously this will not be necessary if the roof has been replaced in recent years as the tiles can be reused. Clay roof tiles have a life expectancy for approximately 60 years. After this time they become brittle, and can easily break if trying to remove them. Slate tiles have a much longer life expectancy for around 90 years. The cost of scaffolding around a three bedroom semi-detached house can cost as much as £1,500.00 so it's something you only want to do once. Ask your builder to ascertain the age of the roof tiles and ask whether they are ok to re-use. If the answer is no ensure you get an accurate price of the works before agreeing. I personally would also recommend replacing the Fasica, Soffit and guttering while the scaffold is up too. It's a relatively

inexpensive job that not only makes the kerb appeal of the house much better, but it's a very common issue for a mortgage surveyor to pick holes is, therefore leading to a lower offer on the property.

There are many variations of loft conversions. You only have to drive around your local area to see the different roof shapes of what used to be identical properties. If your property is semi-detached, the architect would ordinarily design what's called a "Hip to Gable" loft conversion. This is where the side slope of the roof gets removed and a wall is built in its place directly off the existing exterior wall. This is called a gable wall. The very top of the roof called the ridge would then get extended across to meet it. A box like structure known as a Dormer is then added to the rear section of roof. This creates a useable room within the loft space allowing for maximum head height.

Mid-terraced properties already have gable walls. These are the walls in the loft adjoining your neighbouring properties. Because of these, the cost of a loft conversion in a mid-terraced house can be considerably cheaper.

In some instances the standing height in a loft space is not quite enough to allow for a loft conversion. If this is the case then the ceiling joists in the first floor of your property can be lowered thus allowing for a greater head height in the loft. Ask your builder or architect to confirm this with you, as it will cause great disruption to all the upstairs rooms.

Kitchen Extending

Kitchen extensions are one of my favourite alterations on a property. If done correctly it really can give the wow factor to a home. It is said that the kitchen is the heart of the home. If you have ever had a house party I'm sure you will agree it's where everyone congregates. We used to have great house parties when I was growing up and there would often be about 20 people stood in our very small 3m x 2m kitchen.

Where possible I will always do a pitched roof extension with electric roof windows and bi-folding doors. The bi-fold doors bring the outside in and the roof windows open with the touch of a button and make a huge difference to the feel of a room. The pitched roof gives a sense of space and height to a room. Many people are put off by flat roofs, myself included. For one it increases the price of your home insurance, as they are more prone to leak than pitched roofs. They also can make the room feel very claustrophobic if the ceiling height is too low. In the past I have fitted oak bi-folding doors, but have since gone away from this material. I now use Aluminium doors which require no maintenance. The Oak doors would require constant up keep, needing vanishing yearly. I tend to install Anthracite grey bi-folds. The colour makes a feature of the doors. If you are at all nervous about this colour just stick to white.

It's very important to decide on the layout of the room before commencing work, it will save you time and money in the long run. I tend to run cables for a television in the centre of one of the extension walls. The last thing you want to do is see plastic conduit running up your newly plastered wall.

I have seen examples of kitchen extensions gone wrong. I'm a big believer in removing the entire back wall and supporting with a steel beam so the entire room feels as one. However I have seen some extensions where the owners have just removed the old patio doors, keeping the original opening, to save the expense of a steel beam and wall removal. It makes the extension seam very separate from the rest of the house, almost like you have just stuck a box on the back of the property. Where possible avoid this method. The cost of removing the back wall of a house and installing a RSJ is approximately £2,000.00 and you will easily make that money back when you come to sell.

When planning your bi-fold door opening size, be aware of the door cost. The larger the opening the more expensive the doors will be. On average the cost of Aluminium bi-fold doors are £1,200 per Meter so ensure you budget this in to your costing's. If you were building the extension on the rear of an average size three bed semidetached property I would say a 2500mm – 3000mm opening is ample.

One thing to consider before you commence work is your floor covering. The reason I say this is because it can affect the architect's drawings. If you wanted a solid oak flooring which needs nailing down, then it's no good have a concrete sub base. You would need to instruct your architect to design a suspended timber floor into your build to allow for nailing. This doesn't apply to tiled of floating floors. You can see how pre-planning is very important.

Lighting is also important in any development, and pitched roof lighting is no exception. I don't believe in installing spot lights in pitched roofs. Building regulations wouldn't allow this anyway as there is insulation on the underside of your roof rafters. Let me explain. An average a pitched roof rafter size on a 3.5m extension is approximately 175mm in depth. Building regulations stipulates that the roof needs 150mm insulation between the rafters, allowing a 25mm air gap above. Then a further 50mm of insulation on the underside. A spotlight would then get drilled into the ceiling penetrating the insulation making it ineffective. My advice to you is this. Install a hanging pendant in-between each roof window and the outer walls. For example - if you had two roof lights in your ceiling, you would need three pendants. If you had three roof windows you would need four pendants and so on. I personally would purchase lamp shades for these, as a blub on its own can get lost is such a space. If installing the grey bi-fold doors, maybe get a colour lampshade to match. It will tie in nicely.

Radiator positions within the extension can be a tricky one to workout. Anywhere else in a property I would suggest installing them under the window. The window wall would rarely house any furniture as it would limit access to the window. Putting a radiator in the centre of an extension wall can limit your layout. I have found tall slim-line radiators very useful. When there is a steel holding up the back of the property there will be a brick column either side holding it up. These columns are usually about 700mm in width, Perfect for a 500-600mm tall slim-line radiator. Problem solved.

Side Extending

If you are lucky enough to already own a property with a side plot of land or fortunate enough to purchase one, you will be pleased to know it's an incredibly easy way of extending and making large profits. The easiest way to make money is to add square footage and a side extension is no exception. If designed well, you will be able to add an additional reception room, utility room and small garage room on the ground floor and an additional bedroom with en-suite upstairs. There are alternative layouts such as two bedrooms upstairs if you don't add an en-suite, but be careful you don't have too many bedrooms for the amount of bathrooms a property needs.

My recommendation is that a four bedroom house has one main bathroom on the first floor, with at least one en-suite. Ideally it would also have a toilet on the ground floor.

Ensure that when instructing an architect to carry out a set of drawings, you specify exactly what you want. I recently looked at a set of drawings an inexperienced architect had drawn up for a client. It was a double story side extension. The client had asked for more space, well that goes without saying with any extension. However, what he had drawn was crazy and such a waste of money. The property was a three bed semi with and existing attached garage on the side. On the ground floor he had detailed to build on top of the existing garage, leaving it exactly as it was. On the first floor he planned to knock the smallest bedroom wall down, and utilise the space in the new extension to make a massive L shaped bedroom and to enlarge the family bathroom. Well you might as well write a cheque out for £50,000.00 and shove it where the sun doesn't shine because that would have been a complete waste of money. I personally don't think the property would have increased in value at all, let alone earning the £50,000.00 back.

This is what I would have done. I would have divided up the garage on the ground floor into three sections, divided easily with a stud wall, keeping the first third as garage space. Nobody puts cars in garages anymore so there is no need for it to be full depth. I would then utilise the second third of the garage as a downstairs toilet and utility room which would be accessible via the kitchen which would then become larger due to the last third of the garage.

On the first floor I would make an opening at the top of the staircase (so the exits off the stairs now goes left and right) leading into a master bedroom with an en-suite bathroom. I would also still be able to increase the size of the family bathroom. So for the same cost as the original plan I would have increased the property to a four bedroom, one of which has an en-suite, added a utility room, downstairs toilet, larger kitchen and a more generous family bathroom. In that particular part of London the property would have increased by £125k - £150k. That's a profit margin of between £75k - £100k. Not bad for 10 weeks work where the only thing you had to do was make a few cups of tea every so often. It really is that easy. Remember adding a bedroom/s will always increase a property's value. It's one of the easiest ways to make money in property developing.

If your side plot of land is wide enough to maintain an access route to the garden then it's a great idea to maintain that. It will increase the saleability of the property. Not everyone wants to drag all their garden waste through the house. I understand it's not always possible but just keep it in mind.

Fully Refurbishing

Full refurbishments are exactly what it says on the tin. You will need to replace and renovate just about everything in or around the property. I would still be adding square footage with a loft conversion or kitchen/side extension where all the above chapters apply.

You usually find that these houses are in probate, as sadly an elderly person has either passed away or being looked after in a care home and they need to sell the house to pay for their care. When viewing these types of property please bear in mind the feelings of the relatives, as this can be a very difficult and challenging time for them.

If the property hasn't been modernised for many years, you will need to factor in the following costs.

Full re-wire including new consumer unit (Fuse box),

New central heating system, including a new boiler and radiators. I personally would install a combination boiler. They are reasonable in price and very efficient to run.

New windows. Other than aluminium bi-fold doors, I would install white uPVC windows. Again they are very energy efficient and substantially cheaper than aluminium. Stay away from Brown uPVC windows as they make the kerb appeal less attractive. If you are renovating a property that has original wooden sash windows, I would highly recommend re fitting uPVC sash windows. Unlike wooden sash windows there is no maintenance to consider. Please check with your local authority to insure there is no planning permission needed when replacing wooden windows. Bizarre as this sounds, you would be surprised how many window replacements do require permission.

New roof. As described in the loft conversion chapter, roof tiles don't last forever. There are so many varieties of roof tile, all with different life expectancies.

Re-plastering. I re-plaster every square inch of any property I renovate and develop. Without doing so you will never get that crisp finish. Ensure all skirting boards and architraves are removed and replaced with new once the plastering has been completed. If possible allow the plaster to completely dry before fitting any wood work. I also leave skirting and architraves in the property for at least 48 hours to allow the moisture content to adjust. This will limit movement once the woodwork has been fitted. After plastering ensure you allow for bathrooms, kitchen, flooring, decorating etc.

It's the only way to insure a top quality finish. I go as far as ripping out the old wooden internal doorframes and replacing them with new ones. To the untrained eye they might seem fine, but years of wear and tear and copious layers of paint make them look tatty. It will also aid you when fitting new doors, as door sizes have changed over the years with the Metric Imperial changeover.

When fully refurbishing a property, it will be extremely hard to live in. If it's your only property I would advise you to stay with friends or family. At least at the beginning when the major dirty and dusty work is being carried out. It actually will save you money doing it all in one go. Trying to keep a working kitchen and bathroom during the refurbishment will be nigh on impossible and will mean the development will take twice as long.

Plan a system of work from top to bottom, working out what trades you need and when you will need them. Good planning will be cost effective. By having everything ready for each trade, will enable them to make fewer visits hence saving you money. On average a tradesperson will charge approximately £150.00 per day, so the fewer days they need to work the better.

Gardens and Driveway

I'm a huge fan of driveways. If I'm renovating a family home it's a must. In London a well-designed driveway can add as much as £50,000.00 to a property's value. On a typical three bed semi I would say it would increase the value of your property between £15,000.00 – £20,000.00. The number of cars on the road is ever increasing and parking is becoming big business.

Over the years I have designed and built hundreds of driveways ranging from £2,000.00 all the way up to £25,000.00. The average build cost per square meter of a good quality block paving drive is £85.00. As always, make sure you find a reputable tradesperson to carry out the work. Where possible get recommendations from friends and neighbours. What you don't want to happen is that once completed it begins to sink. I guarantee if you took a ten minute walk around your local streets you would see a handful of driveways that haven't been done properly. The reason they tend to sink is because the builders haven't dug down deep enough and not supplied enough sub base material.

There are hundreds of driveway blocks to choose from and they don't always appear the same in the flesh as the glossy brochures lead you to believe. My advice is to take a trip to your local builder's merchants, where you can physically pick the blocks up, ensuring you like them. Make sure you pick blocks that suit the style of your property. Picking a rustic cottage type driveway block can look a little out of place on a modern property. The pictures in the brochure should help you decide. They usually have the picture of the house in the background. Once completed a good quality drive can massively improve the appearance of your home.

Please be careful of picking the cheapest driveway blocks. They are cheap for a reason. The colours can fade in a short space of time and can make the front of your property look tacky. I don't stand for the attitude of "well I'm selling it so it doesn't matter". I want to walk away from a refurbishment knowing I've done the best job possible. I want to be proud of all my refurbishments and you should too.

Gravel is a very cheap and easy drive to lay but please bear in mind who your potential buyers may be. The reason I say this is because pushing a buggy or wheelchair on gravel is impossible. If you are aiming your property towards a young family who have small children, it's a no go. Children also have a tendency to pick things up and put place it in their mouths.

One design aspect I feel I should mention is greenery. Without plants or grass the front garden can easily look a bit like a car park. Try to allow for this in your design; it can also save you large sums of money. Think about where a car is going to sit on the drive and pave that area. Remember to allow for large cars and not just for a Mini. The area around it can be filled with colourful plants or grass. Grass being much cheaper of course. Why spend £85.00 per square meter on something a car isn't going to sit on when grass is £5.00 per square meter. If you are unsure of designs, take a walk around your neighbourhood to get inspiration.

The Best Way to Sell Your Development

You have done months of hard work and planning and it all comes down to this. Selling.

Good marketing and accurate pricing is vital when selling your development. Ensure you get at least three different estate agents around to value your property. I once had a local estate agent value one of my properties at £350,000.00 and it sold for £415,000.00. Had I have gone with that agent; it would have lost me £65,000.00. Ensure the agent has a good reputation, one way to find this out is by looking at how many SOLD signs they have up outside local properties.

Estate agents percentage fee is always negotiable. I have never paid the first percentage they have offered me. Remember they want to sell your property so make sure it's worthwhile for you.

In recent years online estate agents have been increasingly popular due to the fact they offer a set fee regardless of the property value. Some fees are as low as £300 to market your property. They ensure the property is photographed well and is uploaded to all the major online property selling websites.

You can choose to show potential buyers around a property yourself or pay for an agent to assist. Personally I like to show potential buyers around myself. I feel that I would know more about my development than any agent, should a buyer have any questions to ask. Remember to ask people politely to remove their shoes. The last thing you want is a load of dog s**t trod into your new carpets. It also shows that you have respect for the property.

Open days are the new craze and I totally understand why. I have attended many open days myself as a buyer and it certainly makes you understand the competition. It ensures potential buyers put in their highest offer straight off.

I once attended an open day where there were 30 people in one property, it was more like a party than a viewing. The only thing that was missing was the fancy dress and alcohol. I looked around at all these people, trying to listen in to their conversations. I wanted to know would they offer. If so how much? You could feel the tension in the room, everyone was out for themselves. I was later told that out of the 15 couples, 12 had offered, which lead to a bidding war. A war I was not willing to participate in. It was great for the sellers because it meant they got an amazing price for their property but it was too much for what I was willing to pay. That is why it's vital to do your sums, if you get carried away in a bidding war, you could be throwing away your profits.

Furnishing a property to sell has pros and cons and is actually very difficult to get right. It can give potential buyers a great in-site into how the property could look. However it is very easy to clutter a property, making the rooms look small. If you have ever viewed a new build property show home, you will find that they furnish it with the bare minimum. I have never seen a wardrobe in any show home I have ever visited. You also tend to find that the furniture they do have is not full size. A clever but very cheeky furnishing technique.

If you have decided to furnish your property to sell, ensure the furniture you use is neutral and un offensive. Not everyone may like your taste in furniture so try and appeal to the masses.

I really hope you have found this short easy read book useful and I genuinely wish you every success in your new property developing venture.

Remember to be proud of each and every development you complete and don't forget to enjoy it.

Good Luck

Robert Colvin

With over 17 years' experience in property development and renovation Robert Colvin has successfully built up a portfolio of high quality refurbishments and conversions.

"Getting up in the morning, doing a job you love seems an unlikely dream for many, but for the last 17 years that dream for me has been a reality. Renovating a tired dilapidated property is an exciting and pleasurable experience that not only rewards you with gratification but large financial gain.

I believe that whether you'd like a hands on approach to property development, or happy to take a step back and watch your project take shape, with my guidance there are large profits to be made for each and every one of you.

With demand for property in the UK exceeding supply, Property Development is a great way to increase your income, become mortgage free or even become a millionaire.

www.ingramcontent.com/pod-product-compliance
Lightning Source LLC
Chambersburg PA
CBHW072300170526
45158CB00003BA/1128